FOR MUMS

HOW TO LOOK GOOD, STAY SANE AND LIVE AN ENRICHED LIFE

RUCHA DIXIT

WHY I WROTE THIS BOOK

Does your life seem mechanical? Spending 15 minutes having a hot shower feels like a spa treatment. The bathroom seems to be the best place to have a chat with a friend on the phone without being interrupted with teary complaints and untimely toilet trips. Emails, SMS, and rare phone calls appear to be the best methods to communicate with your husband — thanks to technology! Ten minutes to have your cup of tea is luxury. Simple things like eating your meal, leaving the house and watching television are a challenge. Being at work is so much more relaxing. Theatre, movies and dinners with your better half sound like events from a bygone era. Finally, you realise what it means to have your own time and what PEACE is.

Does this sound like your life? Well, then you have all the symptoms of newly acquired Motherhood! And you are not alone.

I'm sure you are glad to hear that. Many of us, myself included, were very much in that place. But I have managed to recuperate from it quite well. Giving birth to two kids has changed my life in numerous ways. It's not only the birth of two new lives, which are now an intrinsic part of mine; it's also the birth of a mother.

Rucha Dixit

Motherhood is undoubtedly one of the most pleasurable experiences of my life. Not only has it revealed various aspects of my personality, but it has also been a teacher in many ways.

Playing the role of a working mother has challenged my patience, tolerance, and physical and mental strength to the limit. Oh yes, children — especially young children — hold PhDs in pushing all your buttons at the same time. As it stands, my children are very young, aged five-and-a-half and three years old. I am a software engineer, working 4 days a week for a multinational company. Life is quite busy, as you can imagine, but I still manage to hit the gym twice a week and meditate at least 4 times a week, thanks to my husband, who has always encouraged me to have my own time. I love staying in shape, and of course I have to give credit to my kids for helping me in that by keeping me on my toes. Even now, I have my "not in a great mood" moments, to put it politely, but I am human and I allow myself to feel what I feel and move on.

Call it nature's instinct or adaptation to circumstances, but being a mother has taught me a lot of things, including how to manage my time efficiently and make the most of it, to be patient, to learn from my kids, to see the futility of anger, to persevere, to let go, to find happiness in the smallest moments and to appreciate life! And this is an attempt to share precisely that, in the knowledge that it will resonate with you and in the hope that it will inspire and motivate you to embrace motherhood with your magnificence.

If you are a mother with young children, short on time, wanting to lose weight but not knowing how to go about doing that, then this book is for you. If you would like to know how to conduct yourself better as a parent, preserve your sanity, and manage your kids better, then you will love this book.

If you would love to be the best possible version of yourself, both as a woman and as a mother, then you should read it.

The repertoire of topics covered in this book comes from a place of honest and practical experience. Their intent is to give mothers what they need: a solution to common problems all mothers go through. The initial chapters of the book walk through the changes that a new mother goes through and are meant to encourage her and help her take charge of the situation and turn it around for her good. This is followed by guidance for dealing with weight issues and techniques to manage her mind and time to make life easy. Then I move on to parenting tips and opening oneself to learning from children. I have also endeavoured to emphasise how meditation can benefit both children and mothers, how parents contribute to creating this world in which we all exist, and how they can present a positive influence. I recommend reading it with an open mind.

Rucha Dixit

I have braved this enjoyable chaos and madness to write this book, bit by bit, every night. I hope this gives you a boost of inspiration to carry on playing the most vital role of your life — as a mother. And if it does, it has made all the effort worthwhile!

TABLE OF CONTENTS

CHAPTER 1. LIFE CHANGES

Change is something everyone fears. But as they say, the only constant thing in life is change. Change is inevitable and more so with motherhood, it is also humongous.

Nobody likes the idea of being pushed out of their comfort zone and to their limits. And parenthood does just that, especially if it's the first time you are having a baby. One fine day, your baby is out and your world has changed. The good news is that it's for the better, but the bad news is that it also has the not-so-good bits tagged with it. It's a world of duality, you see. Even though both mother and father are in it together, it's the mother who is hit harder by the not-so-good bits. And that's because it's an investment of her body and mind for much more than nine months.

After having kids, every aspect of my life has undergone transformation. My body, mind, priorities, perspective, and relationships...nothing has been spared from change. But the sooner I accepted and embraced that, the easier it became for me to cope. I guess I just dropped the mental barrier and let life flow.

Don't get the wrong end of the stick. Being a mother is a blessing and makes my life worth living every moment. No matter how many pain-in-the-backside moments my kids give me, just a smile or a hug from them makes my day. And the worst thing for me would be to see them hurt in any way.

I still remember the first time I held my son, my firstborn. It was after twenty hours of labour that the midwife placed him on my chest. At that very moment, I wasn't emotional, just blank. It's probably that when emotions get very overwhelming, you cease feeling anything at all. Such a fragile little life. He tilted his tiny head and looked me straight in the eye.

The feeling of being a mother sank in days later and my motherly protective instincts surfaced. I noticed myself getting very touchy with little things, like someone holding my baby in a way that made him uncomfortable. A little cry from him in any corner of the house would set me off running to see if everything was okay. Having heard some horror stories would compel me to wake up many times at night to check on him. My husband used to jokingly call me "Tigress."

After having my baby, everything revolved around him, or it seemed so. Meals interrupted by baby feeding, diaper changing or puke accidents were a norm. On every social invitation, the first concern was not what dress I would wear, but what I had packed in my baby bag and making sure that I had enough baby food and extra clothes to deal with emergencies. Looking great wasn't a priority; being comfortable was.

For someone like me who had always looked lean and slender her whole life, going from a body-fat percentage of twenty-one to thirty-one was painful. This was psychological feminine pain born out of the helplessness of having a wardrobe full of smashing outfits and not being able to fit in any of them anymore, thanks to the sagging waistline, chubby arms and big belly. It was hard to believe that this was the same body I had always been in all these years. Moreover, the lower back pain, swinging moods, baby blues, hormonal changes and weakness made it even more difficult.

Life had changed in a big way. Every time I walked into the room, my baby's eyes would lock onto me and follow me wherever I went. My sister called him "Mum Flower!" All of a sudden, there was a new tiny being in my life and I was perfect to him the way I was. I was in love again with the second man in my life. The days my son didn't eat well, I and my husband felt guilty about having our own meals. We had become parents now in every aspect.

Then, after two and a half years, my daughter entered the family. A born smiler, she gave me a smile as early as two weeks! Now, this didn't seem as easy as one-plus-one-makes-two. That equation didn't seem to fit here because the responsibility and work seemed to have multiplied. Having two kids was an entirely different ball game. After having my first child, life changed, but the magnitude of it was incomparable to

3

when I had my second. My son was only two-and-a-half years old when she was born. He took it quite well for his age, but they don't call them "Terrible Twos" without a reason. My busy time with my new baby frustrated him as he sought my attention, and it came out in annoying ways.

After two kids, suddenly there was no time even for a casual chat with my husband, let alone discussing important matters. After I was through with the frustration of attempts to talk to him amidst screaming children that resulted in no conclusions, I turned to technology, my saviour. I landed up communicating with him on email. Sometimes, this left me feeling teary as I missed the days I had his undivided attention and time. Thankfully, it's better now that the kids are older.

Even now, I face disruptions during meal times, but the frequency has gone down and the reasons are more evolved — mainly being untimely toilet trips, wars as a result of sibling rivalry, tantrums and accidents as a consequence of mischievous geniuses working overtime. At least the diaper phase is now done with, so no carrying baby bags around.

On the work front, I have reduced my working hours by 20 percent. Now, my workday is six hours, which effectively overlaps with school hours. That gives me the energy to juggle both home and work and also the satisfaction and balance of having a life of my own and giving time to my kids.

Being a mother has helped me understand people around me. It's probably because my imagination has taken a motherly bent, and even though my kids aren't teenagers yet, I can understand how my parents would have felt when I behaved in certain not-so-kind ways as a teenager, and how I shouldn't have taken my mother for granted. It's like seeing the world in a new light. On the flip side, it looks like I can also understand my mother-in-law better. Now that's an achievement!

So, as you can see, my life changed radically after having my children, both for good and bad. But it is up to you, really, to choose if you want to lose yourself amongst all the chaos and feel despair or embrace the changes, work through them and regain yourself again. I chose the latter.

In the chapters to follow, I will share my approach, but before that I would like you to face your fears and get into the right frame of mind.

Chapter 2. Putting Things In Perspective

"To change your future, change your present."
- Swami Vivek Anand

I have known women with young children and have noticed their desire to do a lot more with their lives, like lose weight, get some time to themselves, do a course, pursue a hobby...the list goes on. Mostly these aren't radically ambitious targets, but motherhood is equally as challenging as it is pleasurable and it can be tricky to find the right balance between being a good mother and finding yourself again.

Are you a mother who wants to lose weight and fit in one of those sexy dresses hanging in your wardrobe from the pre-baby days? Every time you look at it, you tell yourself that someday you will get into it. And probably you promise yourself to go on a salad-only diet the whole of next week. Then, next week, you are invited to a party and you forget the promise you made to yourself! Or are you someone who thinks it's okay to be chubby because now you are a mother and that's how mothers are meant to look? Somewhere in the corner of your mind, you know that's an excuse you are giving yourself.

If any of the above sounds familiar, then its time you faced the enemy. It's right in your face and you can't see it, can you? The enemy is the resistance your mind creates that stands in the way. The first time I noticed this was when I joined a yoga class a few months after giving birth to my first child. The yoga instructor used to get us into these postures where discomfort was inevitable and then ask us to observe the resistance created by the mind. "Don't let your mind tell you that you can't do it," she used to say. "Just observe it and let go."

Remember that "Someday" will never come unless you make it happen. The only thing that keeps you from your goal is your own mind. It's your ego that tells you that you are not good enough to acquire what you truly desire. Blaming your circumstances and the thought that having kids is keeping you from it is another trick your ego plays on you.

I know what you are thinking: "Where do I find the time?" I agree that time is going to be a rare commodity if you are a new mother, but "having time" is more of an attitude than a fact. Moreover, thinking you don't have time is another form of resistance. It wasn't until after having two kids that I realised how much time I actually had on my hands before I had them. Sometimes I just think of the endless list of things I could have learnt and invested time in. But we don't really value things when

we have them, and if we do at all, it's in retrospect.
That's a classic human trait we are all familiar with.

I have seen women with two kids pursuing their MBAs,
and I have also seen women with minimal
responsibilities who don't have time to even cook. It
isn't about having kids or not. It's about what you want
to do and what you are telling yourself. Whether you
think you have time or not, either way, you are right!

Bestselling author Doreen Virtue wrote her first book as
a mother of two young kids, with a day job and whilst
attending college. J.K. Rowling, one of the wealthiest
women in the world thanks to the success of her Harry
Potter series, just two decades ago was a struggling
single mom, feeling like a failure. These examples
represent the pinnacle of human potential. If this is
possible, then why is Little Old You holding on to the "I
don't have time for this" syndrome?

The point is that these people are human and so are
you. Say you and your friend had exactly the same
mobile phone model and she showed you how a certain
feature on it worked, which you were unaware of.
Wouldn't you try and explore it on your phone, now
that you know that your phone is capable of it?

I am not suggesting neglecting your responsibilities as a
mother to do what it is that you want to. All I am trying
to say is that if you really want to do something, you will
find a way to do it, and if you don't, you will find an

excuse. Only you are stopping yourself and only YOU are the person who can help yourself.

FINDING TIME

Are you making excuses about not having time?

We don't actually realise how much time we waste. You have to choose what matters to you.

Try this exercise. For the next week, make it a point to write down all your activities on paper. Here is an example.

<u>Day 1</u>

- Had breakfast
- Ready for work
- Get kids ready for school/nursery
- Commute on train
- Lunch with a friend
- Return commute back home
- Cook dinner
- Put kids to bed
- Sleep time

This is what my day might look like. Even on a weekday, from the example above you can see that I have some time to myself when I have my train commute. I use it to read books or to meditate. I have a little time after the kids go to bed, which I am currently using to write this book. Even if you are a mother who is breastfeeding, you still have the time while you are feeding your baby. When you do this for a week, you will see yourself having time. This will shift your focus from "not having time" to "having time."

You will also find that we spend time socialising, which is not always necessary. You don't have to be a recluse, but you have to identify what matters most. Prioritisation is the keyword. You might need to let go of things you like to do the things you LOVE. There are things you like and there are things you love. There is a difference. I like mangoes but I don't wait desperately all year around for the season to arrive, thinking about them. In fact, I wouldn't miss not eating them for even months. But I love to stay fit and I just can't stand the thought of getting fat. That's why I make it a point to hit the gym at least twice a week, no matter what. So if you have to drop out of certain social events and occasions to find time for yourself and pursue your passion, then why not? Learn to do so unapologetically. People who really love you will understand, support and appreciate you for this.

DON'T LABEL YOURSELF

Catch yourself when you say something like, "I could never do that." or "I don't have that much determination to lose weight." Labelling yourself like this does more damage than good. In fact, it's like putting an end to everything you want. If you think negatively in your head, how the hell are you going to bring about positive results? You are only demoralising yourself and, again, finding an excuse to not achieve your goal. I have known so many people who get into a vicious circle where they feel bad for not doing what they want to do, label themselves for lacking determination and, again, feel bad about themselves. If you are in one, it's high time you jumped out NOW.

Do this clearing exercise if you are desolate or hopeless over something. Take a piece of paper and write down all the negative thoughts you have about yourself. Let them come out on paper as strongly as you feel them. So if you think you are not good enough or lack determination, just write it. Then rip this piece of paper to bits and bin them. This is like chucking away all your negativity physically. Now, take new paper and write down how you would like yourself to be, the ideal version of yourself that you envision. This way, you have discarded your negativity and emphasised the positives. The pull of negativity is very strong, so beware of getting into a habit of pitying yourself and enjoying it! Just don't allow yourself to sink into negativity. I would suggest doing this whenever you feel down.

START WITH THE GOAL IN MIND

What most of us do is focus on the undesirable situation we are in—that is, what we don't want—and then feel a lack of motivation, courage and discipline to get working towards eliminating it. I am asked so many times how I managed to lose so much weight, and how I stay motivated to hit the gym so regularly, and how do I not get bored of it. The answer is that I visualised the end result. When I decided to lose weight, I focused on the slimmer, fitter and healthier form of myself, and that keeps me going.

Start with the end goal in mind and then work backwards towards how you can achieve it. This starts you off on a positive note and keeps you enthused.

BOOK TIME FOR YOURSELF IN YOUR CALENDAR

If you really want to do something, then start by committing to dedicate time to it regularly. This will help you move ahead, even if it is at a slow pace, but it's better than not making any progress.

Let's take my example. I am a working woman with two kids, and I don't really need to stress the fact that life is busy. But I love to write, and I really want to write and complete this book. Making it happen is in my hands alone, and therefore I have made a commitment to myself to write at least 500 words every day. Some days I manage to write more than 500, which is a bonus, but I try my level best to keep the commitment. It's like an eye test appointment at an optician. If you have it booked in your calendar, then you will go anyway, whether you want to or not.

Once you start doing this, you will see how it changes you gradually. If you do feel lazy, it's okay.

Commitments are meant to be outside one's comfort zone, and only by stretching yourself slightly can you grow. I have seen that if I feel lazy at times about keeping my promise to write 500 words and I don't do it, I feel worse. It doesn't feel good, which defeats the purpose of skipping it, right? But believe me; even if you feel lazy at the start, stick to your commitment and you will see how the immense sense of satisfaction you experience after you go ahead is indescribable. It also proves to you that you are stronger than those gremlins in your mind which are holding you back.

All this is to impel you, but I don't want you to tip the scale beyond a certain point. Some people are very driven from within, so much so that they take on too much and ruin everything in the process. Keeping the balance is crucial. So although this is to get you to be driven, which is an asset to have, don't forget to enjoy the journey on the way. Don't forget to live!

Chapter 3. How To Shape Up And Look Good

For centuries, the female community has been seduced into looking beautiful. This cultural and social conditioning starts at a very young age and the media only adds to it. Photographs of these picture-perfect models (thanks to makeup and Photoshop) have gone viral all over: in magazines, on billboards, in commercials and on the Internet. This puts so much pressure and stress on women because it reminds them of their physical imperfections and creates an intense desire to look like these models. No wonder so many juvenile girls are suffering from anorexia.

What is beauty? If you ask an Asian, fair skin is beautiful—the whiter, the better. But if you ask a European, brown skin is in! It's all relative. We don't appreciate what we have. A woman with curly hair secretly envies the naturally pin-straight, silky tresses of another woman, and the converse is true, too. Even the celebrity goddess you worship as the epitome of beauty thinks she is not perfect.

Moreover, this only highlights the body consciousness we all are stuck with, the identification of ourselves with our bodies instead of our spirits. Beauty comes from within, it comes from the soul. It is being real, natural and accepting of what you are, the way you are. But it also means taking care of what you have been blessed with, the temple of your soul. Your body!

All this is to tell you that you are beautiful. God doesn't create garbage! My intention is NOT to tell you how to be a size zero to look beautiful, but to tell you how to be healthy and fit even if you end up a curvy UK size 12.

So, coming back to the point, once you are aware that it's the resistance of your own mind that stands in your way, you are on the path, already heading in the right direction! That's half the job done. Now it's time to take action.

After having my first child, I was 15 kilos overweight. I stand 5 feet and 9 inches tall and have always been around 62 kilos. But hitting 77 kilos on the scale was a shocker! Moreover, it was the first time something like this had ever happened to me.

Here are the steps I took to lose that weight in a year. They are not in any order necessarily, just points to keep in mind. And they are proven to work, because I have done it twice. After my second baby, I was in fact 20 kilos overweight and I lost the excess weight successfully. But I state all this on the assumption that you are in perfect health, without any underlying health conditions that might have caused your weight gain. If that's not the case, then it is advisable to see a doctor.

BE REAL

Make realistic goals. Don't take an oath to not touch ice cream and chocolates your whole life. That creates a mental burden and you most likely will heavily indulge again. Start off with short-term targets. Just promise yourself to eat healthy for the next three days. Gradually increase this commitment to a week. Eventually, you will build a discipline of eating right.

SHIFT YOUR ATTENTION

It's a human tendency to focus on the unwanted instead of thinking about the wanted. But just because the majority of the population does it, doesn't mean it's normal. Whatever you put your attention on grows. So focus on the desired results.

Start off by weighing yourself so you know where you are right now. But I wouldn't recommend having a target as specific as "I want to lose 12 kilos in 18 months." This keeps the focus on wanting to lose weight instead of being healthy and fit. Put all your attention on how you would like to see yourself and not on "losing weight."

Just start and see how you feel. After a month, I am sure you will get positive feedback from people around you, and maybe then you can weigh yourself. That will give you starting motivation, because you'll have significant and noticeable results in front of you. This is better than weighing yourself every week, stressing about what the scale will show you and focusing on weight loss instead of the fitter, healthier YOU.

EXERCISE

You can't cheat success. You have to do the work. Regular exercise is a must even when you don't want to lose weight. I work out for 45 minutes to an hour at least two times a week now to maintain my weight. But when I was trying to lose weight, I used to work out three to four times a week.

1. SEEK PROFESSIONAL ADVICE

When I decided to lose weight, I first consulted a doctor, which is what I would recommend. I was told not to work out for at least 6 months post-delivery to give my body enough time to convalesce.

I was used to working out in the gym before I had babies, so this wasn't something which was new to me. Even then, I got a proper gym instructor to create a training program to suit my situation at that time. I gave them all the facts, like I told them that I was there to get toned and fit and lose weight, that I had lower back pain and wanted to target my belly fat. It's safer to take professional guidance instead of directing yourself.

2. STARTING EXERCISE

Even if you have been used to working out or been very active at sports or been very fit physically prior to having a baby, you don't want to start off with a big bang just in case you injure your joints. During pregnancy, the placenta produces a hormone called *relaxin*. As the name implies, relaxin loosens and relaxes the body's muscles, joints, and ligaments. This is in preparation for labour. But even post-birth, your body will carry high levels of relaxin for up to six months or even longer if you are breastfeeding. And this is why coming back to exercising should be easy and gradual.

When I started off, I just walked on the treadmill at a moderate speed for 20 minutes for the first few days. I was amazed at how I got back my stamina within two weeks. The body sure has memory! It might take you shorter or longer than this. It's okay, we are all different and unique in our own ways. Take your time to settle in your new workout regime.

3. EXERCISE ROUTINE

Three, 1 hour workouts a week are a must, especially if you are trying to burn extra fat. But start gradually. Do a combination of cardio and weight training. With weight training, you can do both free weights and machine weights because of the way they differ. Unlike machine weights, free weights help you work against gravity, which is why you can handle more weight on a machine than you can in free weights.

Fitness trainers recommend spending typically 25 to 30 minutes doing cardio and 30 minutes in weight training and floor exercises. Don't worry about looking like a WWE wrestler. Trust me; it's not that easy to bulk up. In fact, weight training gives your body a toned look, increases bone density and helps to take your love handles away.

Also, try alternating between cardio and weight training. For instance, go 15 minutes on the treadmill, followed by two minutes of rest. Then spend 15 minutes doing floor exercises, followed by 15 minutes on the bike. Again, rest for five minutes and then spend 15 minutes with free weights and on the strength training machines.

Doing bursts of high-intensity cardio followed by low-intensity cardio helps you lose fat quickly. For example, run for a minute on the treadmill at a speed of 12 and then walk for a minute at a speed of 6. Repeat five to six times. But make sure you warm up well before running at high speed, else you might damage your ligaments and tendons.

Another thing to try is varying your workout every six to eight weeks. This way, you don't let your body settle down into a type of workout; you keep throwing surprises at it, which makes it lose weight.

4. BONUS
A good workout is like getting a facial. What does a facial do? It increases blood circulation to your skin, and so does exercise. Moreover, sweating during exercise flushes out the toxins in the body, resulting in a clearer and blemish-free complexion. My colleague at work once disclosed to me that she lost all her pimples after

regularly sweating it out at the gym. So you can skip the trips to the salon and save that money for something worthwhile. I barely get one facial in a year, if at all.

Exercise releases endorphins, the happy hormone. Don't be surprised if you have a spring in your step the whole day after spending a morning doing yoga or some other form of exercise.

EAT A HEAVY BREAKFAST FIRST THING IN THE MORNING

Never skip breakfast. On the contrary, make sure it's a heavy one but a healthy one. It literally fuels your body's metabolism, which is highest in the morning.

First thing I do every morning after I wake up is drink warm water and then eat something. Most people say that they don't feel like eating first thing after waking up, and so did I when I started. But once you start practising this, you will see that you get hungry as soon as you wake up. It's a healthy sign. After you have eaten, you are free to have that cup of tea.

I would recommend reading a very good book on weight loss called *Don't Lose Your Mind, Lose Your Weight* by Rujuta Diwekar, a celebrity dietician and nutritionist. She explains in this book why it is important to eat something first thing in the morning and have tea or coffee only after that. You can find it at the end of this book in the inspirational books and videos section.

EAT EVERY 2 TO 3 HOURS

Eating about six to seven small meals a day boosts your metabolism. Moreover, it doesn't leave you hungry to then binge on your main meals later in the day. Experts suggest that eating every two to three hours leaves just the right amount of time in between meals and keeps metabolic activity higher in the body as compared to what it would be if you were to have only three main meals. Again, this is something I learnt in the book I mentioned above by Rujuta Diwekar.

Starving to lose weight is worse. Imagine a region hit by a famine. What is the natural reaction to this? The population starts storing food in bulk from rescue operations or any other resource, which they wouldn't have done otherwise but have to now because they aren't sure they will get food tomorrow. Starving is like creating a famine in the body, and this is when the panic alarm goes off. This results in the body storing fat. So the less you eat, the more fat your body stores. But if there is abundance, or should I say a continuous supply of food in the right amount, then the body doesn't feel the need to store excess fat.

You can choose from healthy snacks like cheese strips, roasted nuts, or high-fibre wheat biscuits for these smaller meals.

EAT DINNER EARLY

My instructor at the gym suggested eating dinner early—that is, by 6:30 pm—as that gives your body enough time to digest the food before you hit the bed. Your metabolism falls as the day progresses and is minimal after 9 pm. So, the idea is to not give your body any hard work to do after 9 pm, else it will just be lazy and store that food as fat. Why? Simply because it doesn't have the energy to break it down, as it would have done earlier in the day.

This tip has helped me to drastically cut down on belly fat. My parents were so inspired that they tried it too and have lost oodles of weight, especially on the abdomen, without vigorous exercise (which they can't do anyway at their age). If you feel hungry later at night, you can have something light, like a glass of semi-skimmed milk, or something high in fibre, like a whole-wheat biscuit, oatmeal or whole-wheat toast.

EAT SENSIBLY & GUILT FREE

Extreme diets don't work. Neither have I ever been on one nor do you need to. The weight just comes back on. Stay healthy, eat healthy. Watch what you eat, but don't be obsessed about eating fat-free food or guilty about eating fatty food occasionally. The guilt, again, is a culprit to gaining more weight.

Stop eating the kids' leftovers. You would be surprised how many women do that. A mum is not meant to double for a trash can, and even though your intent toward avoiding the waste of food is very solemn, you are actually abusing your own body.

FAT ISN'T A NO-NO

Eliminating fat from your diet is unnecessary and can actually give you unwanted results. An excessively low-fat diet will rid your skin of its radiance and will give it a weathered, wrinkled look. Opt for healthy fats like oily fish, nuts, cheese and avocados instead of hash browns, fried bacon and eggs. Raw cashews are better than fried ones.

I love eating avocados for breakfast. They give my skin an amazing radiance. It's not really surprising to learn how many facial washes and creams have avocado oil, is it? Why invest in those expensive creams with chemicals in them? Instead, eating healthy is cheaper. Also, it is like injecting the nutrients into your bloodstream straightaway rather than waiting to let them sink in through your skin, so it's far more effective.

TIMING AND QUANTITY ARE IMPORTANT

We live in a real world, and commitments like "I won't eat cake for my whole life" are highly unrealistic. You don't have to do this. Quantity and timing are everything. If you can't resist that piece of cake, eating it first thing in the morning is the best time. That's the time your metabolism is highest, and it's less likely to sit on the wrong places. But, of course, I don't mean *every* morning, nor do I suggest binging on it.

REDUCE STRESS

There are opportunities galore for stress if you have young kids. But beware, as stress releases hormones that retain fat on the abdomen. Try yoga and breathing exercise for a few minutes each day. Meditation can help you to significantly cut down on stress. The next chapter has more on that.

DRINK PLENTY OF WATER

The human body needs at least two litres of water every day. This is a well-known fact and still most of us don't diligently follow it. It can work in your favour like magic, enhancing skin complexion and improving digestion. If you are breastfeeding, then you need at least a litre more than normal each day because you are losing a lot of water feeding your baby.

Drinking warm water if you can is ideal, but if not, then try and drink it at room temperature. Science has proven that drinking warm water half an hour after a meal can help your body break down and digest fat easily, as compared to drinking cold water. Imagine a cake tin greased with butter. What would it look like if you poured cold water on it? That is what you do to your intestinal walls by drinking cold water after a meal.

Drinking plenty of water rids your body of toxins and excess salt, preventing water retention, which can give you a puffy look. You can keep it interesting by drinking green tea high in antioxidants. Dandelion leaf and root tea are excellent options.

Dandelion is an herb, and Dandelion leaf or root teas have a moderate but effective diuretic effect (which means that it prevents water retention) without side effects. They are high in potassium and replace the potassium lost as a result of taking a diuretic. Dandelion is also rich in Vitamins A, C and D. It prevents flatulence and bloating, which can be an issue during breastfeeding. Moreover, it has been known to promote lactation.

Rooibos is another caffeine-free tea that I love. Rooibos tea is beneficial in pregnancy and breastfeeding. It is loaded with antioxidants and also contains calcium and magnesium. It is known to aid digestion and can ease colic and reflux in babies. Children can drink Rooibos, and it tastes great with milk and a little honey. It is also known to help with weight loss.

Before proceeding though, I would suggest checking with your midwife or doctor first, to be safe.

TRICK YOURSELF

Thinking about something complicates it and gives you an illusion of it being too difficult to do. I started taking driving lessons at the age of 18. I still remember how complex driving would appear to me when I used to think about it. I used to wonder how somebody could ever synchronise so many things together. A hand on the gear and another on the wheel, a foot on the clutch and the other foot on the brake and accelerator! Even reading the previous line would make a novice think it's a circus! But is it that difficult? We all do it so easily, and it gets mechanical after a while. Doesn't it?

So don't let your mind fool you. Enrol yourself into exercise classes that charge you extra if you don't show up. Take annual memberships for gyms which make you go as you have paid. That's a trick to kill mental resistance. Don't think. Just do it. Just jump into it, and you will be pleasantly surprised to see how you cope absolutely fine.

TALK TO YOUR BODY

On days where you just can't avoid eating heavy food, at a party or on special occasions and festivals, just tell your body to co-operate with you. Yes! The mind is very powerful. It has been scientifically proven that thoughts travel and can be measured, as they are nothing but frequencies. So you can direct your body with your thoughts. How do you think some people heal others remotely? They do so by directing their thoughts to the subject. If you were to exist a century ago and somebody were to tell you that it was possible to speak to a person tens of thousands of miles away on a little slim box, without even being connected to a wire, you would think that person was nuts! But now having a mobile is the norm, right?

I am telling you a secret. When I am in a situation I can't escape, like being compelled to eat fast food with my kids (which is rare, as I generally don't like and encourage it), I just ask my body to shed the excess fat and not retain it. And it works. Trying it won't hurt, anyway. You have nothing to lose except fat!

VISUALISE AND AFFIRM THE FITTER YOU

We all have some beliefs about everything, including our bodies. If you have a problem area, like a chubby abdomen, where you think you gain weight very quickly or don't lose fat easily from, reiterating those thoughts isn't going to help — but changing those beliefs will.

Whenever a thought like that crosses your mind, just affirm what you want. So here you can say something like, "I have a flat abdomen. I lose weight easily on my stomach." Try repeating it, and every time put as much sentiment into it as possible. I do it every time I exercise. Affirmations are a powerful way of training your subconscious mind to think in a certain way. I have more on this in the next chapter. Uprooting old beliefs takes time, so be patient and persistent with this technique.

BE SINCERE, BUT DO WHAT YOU CAN

Don't be too hard on yourself. If you can't attend that yoga class one day, forgive yourself. Being upset only creates more stress! Instead, you can make it up by dancing with your kids. (Shakira's "Waka Waka" is my favourite.) This way, you get exercise and give them time. But beware of a tendency to forgive yourself too often. Pocket a bit of the guilt if it helps keep you on track. Only a little bit though!

REWARD YOURSELF

This is the best part. Once you start losing weight, don't forget to pat yourself on the back for all the good work and to keep going. Enjoy a sundae, maybe!

I am not obsessed with weight. Even though now I am 64 kilos, which is a few kilos over my pre-pregnancy weight, I don't fuss about it! Also, don't forget that you gain muscle when you work out, so weight doesn't always mean fat; that's why I don't weigh myself very frequently.

When I think back, I never thought about not being able to lose weight. In other words, it just felt natural to be fit and lean, so the thought of remaining overweight my entire life didn't cross my mind. So believe in yourself, because you can't get anywhere otherwise. It's not only about looking slim and toned. It's also about feeling good about one's self. When you feel good, you conduct yourself better.

CHAPTER 4. PRESERVING YOUR SANITY

I was listening to one of Dr. Wayne Dyer's talks on YouTube a few months back. He asked the audience, "What comes out if you squeeze an orange?" and someone replied "Orange juice."

"Yes," he said, "Because that's what is inside."

Raising children isn't easy. It pushes you to the edge, and there are times you feel like pulling your hair with frustration. But when you are squeezed in situations like these, then what you have inside will come out. If you are frustrated and angry, then that is what will come out. And worse, it will come out on your kids — something you will regret later when it's too late, when you can't do anything to change it. I have found that working on your inside can do wonders. It can transform your relationships; it can help you be more peaceful, calmer and happy. If you are happy, then you can give happiness because you can only give what you have. And only happy, contented parents can make happy families. Moreover, I think children tend to derive their emotional strength and support from mothers. So it's crucial as a mother to be sensitive, else

Rucha Dixit

you won't feel what they do, but also strong so you can support them in times of need.

In this chapter, I have tried to bring forward everything that helps me to get through trying times in my ongoing mission as a mother.

MEDITATION

There was a time when I found it very difficult to cope with two kids and it made me very irritable and teary quite often. I felt myself going into lows for really silly reasons; I laugh thinking about them now. All this culminated in migraine headaches. I never had a tendency toward migraines, not even after having my first child. This was a clearly an indication of stress. I didn't need medication. What I needed was to work on my inside, my mind, my spirit.

When the student is ready, the teacher appears. I don't know how I got convinced into trying meditation. My mother had been telling me for years to do it, but I had turned a deaf ear to her until then. I was on maternity leave, so I had some time while my daughter slept, and I thought there was nothing to lose if I gave it a shot. So I started, and saw a difference in myself since then.

I will be honest. No matter how much I try, I am not able to do it daily, but I try to meditate at least four times a week. If I don't for a while, then I start missing it, because I see myself losing patience and getting irritable often. Regular meditation keeps me calmer and more balanced. Let me tell you from my personal experience what advantages you can gain out of meditation:

1. STRESS BUSTER

Every person is surrounded by electromagnetic radiations. Now, many of you might think this is New Age crap. But trust me, it isn't. You can try experiment three in the book *E-Squared: Nine Do-It-Yourself Energy Experiments that Prove Your Thoughts Create Your Reality* by Pam Grout, which proves it. These vibrations affect people around you, and guess who is around you very often? Your kids. A parent's vibes make a huge difference to these young, growing minds that unknowingly absorb them. Meditation changes your aura, cleanses it and raises your vibrations. It reduces stress and uplifts your mood. It's like a dose of anti-depressant.

2. ENERGY BOOSTER

We all know how being a parent can drain your energy. The younger the children, the more they keep you on your toes. Meditation can help you deal with this by recharging your body and mind. It's literally like plugging yourself into a charger. It has been proven that twenty minutes of meditation equals eight hours of sleep, which a good night's sleep is. So if you are having sleepless nights with young children, fifteen minutes in meditation can give you that recharge. You will also notice that the more you meditate, the less you will be affected by sleep deprivation.

3. IMMUNITY BOOSTER

As a mother, you can't afford to fall sick, as not only you but your whole family suffers. I found that meditating regularly kept me away from catching flu as easily as I did earlier. It's definitely an immunity booster. Meditation coupled with breathing exercises or Pranayama works wonders. *Pranayama* means "extension of the life force." It increases lung capacity and helps the body get more oxygen. It also eliminates carbon dioxide more efficiently.

4. INCREASES EFFICIENCY

Scientific studies tell us that we have up to 60,000 thoughts in a day and that 98 percent of these thoughts are repetitive. More significantly, 80 percent of these thoughts are negative. This does not help in any way and blocks us from getting new ideas and being prolific. Meditation settles the mind and calms it down so that we can focus on what we are doing. It increases productivity, enhances creativity and helps you manage your time effectively.

5. ANTI-AGING TREATMENT

Last, but definitely not the least, as this is what most women would kill for! Meditation works as a wonderful anti-aging treatment. Experts say that it revives your skin, reduces the production of free radicals and slows down aging. And the best part is it's free. It doesn't cost you a dime. So ditch those expensive creams and serums. Don't believe me? Try it! You will glow!

As with everything new, you will never know what meditation is unless you try it yourself. It's like, if you haven't attempted swimming ever in your life, unless you get into the water yourself, you won't know what swimming is. No matter how many people you watch swim, or in however much detail I try and describe it to you in words, you won't know what it is. To experience it, you have to get into the water.

So make meditation a part of your life. All you have to do is sit back in a quiet place for just 15 minutes and close your eyes. This is your own quiet time. There are a lot of guided mediation tapes available at your fingertips online, thanks to the evolution of science and technology.

Pick a time that is convenient. I generally stick to 9 pm every night because that's a time my kids are asleep and my husband is buried behind a book. It's just fifteen minutes of your time and it's an investment you will never regret — that's a guarantee! You can even create a meditation room or corner in your house to be your little retreat and dress it with things you like, such as candles or incense sticks.

Finally, it's important to be sincere and meditate whenever and wherever possible, but again, don't be too hard on yourself if you have to break your schedule and just can't make it on certain days. Stressing over it is doing just the opposite of meditation; it's creating more stress.

POSITIVE AFFIRMATIONS

Positive affirmations do wonders by bringing us back to the present moment. They remind us that worrying and stressing about things is a futile exercise.

Most women go through emotional turmoil after birth due to a lot of factors, like physical changes, life changes and hormonal changes. You might worry about coping as a parent, or not being as productive at work as before. Whatever it is, positive affirmations can do wonders. There are numerous books available on the topic you can read out of interest. I am in particular very fond of Louise Hay's books on this subject, which you might want to explore as well. So any time I worry about anything, I say to myself, just like Louise says, "Only good lies ahead of me."

What I find most effective, though, is making mental markers on objects or places that remind you to affirm about things you want to change. If there is something you would like to change in your life — for instance, if it's your tendency to get angry quickly — make a mental marker on the windows of your house. Every time you look at them, say, "Anger is out of the window and my life." That's just an example and it might sound a bit ridiculous, but it's an effective way of reminding yourself and eventually becoming anger-free.

You can find other ways of reminding yourself. Say you think you are good for nothing. Put a recurring reminder in your phone that says, every morning at 9, "I am a No-Limit person." When you read it, say it in your mind a couple of times with feeling. This is truly empowering.

Also, instead of letting your mind go haywire when you are not doing much, like commuting to work on the train, use it for affirming yourself. I generally do this and it has helped me see significant changes in a lot of areas of my life.

Reading good books keeps your vibrations high. I do a lot of inspirational reading on the train. It's a good use of my time.

BREATHE OUT NEGATIVITY

Sri Sri Ravishankar, who is the founder of Art of Living, says that a way of releasing negative emotions is to breathe them out of your system. If you feel you are not confident enough, then breathe in confidence and imagine the opposite, negative sentiment leaving you. Dr. Wayne Dyer suggests breathing out negativity in an imaginary balloon, then just visualising it floating away from you. You don't have to fight it, kill it or overcome it. Just be, and just let it go. It's mentally soothing and relaxing.

ALLOW YOURSELF TO FEEL WHAT YOU FEEL

All this emphasis on positive thinking and the law of attraction (which says you attract what you think) these days can feel like a burden when you are low. So if you are feeling really weighed down by all the stress of handling your kids, this puts you under pressure to feel good all the time and think positive, right?

Firstly, accept that you are feeling bad. Don't force yourself to feel positive. It has to come from within. That's where meditation helps. If you feel like crying, just get it out. There is no shame in doing so. I let myself cry in peace, and then I am done. It's out of my system. Keeping it supressed can be dangerous to your mental and physical health. Talk to friends if you need to vent. If you can't talk, like my friend once told me, write it down or type it out in a Word .doc and delete it. That can take a load off the mind. If you make meditation a habit, you will see your inner strength build up and you will see yourself getting into the lows less and less, so you won't need tears anymore to relieve yourself.

MAKE TIME FOR YOURSELF
Most women think, or are made to think, that motherhood is their prime responsibility. Which it is, but also that they shouldn't be spending time on themselves. This is especially dominant in Asian cultures. Don't buy into collective social thinking that life after kids has to be mundane and that it's about sacrificing completely for your children. Sacrifice can't make you happy.

I have known women who feel guilty for having some time for themselves. Isn't that a ridiculous thought? Motherhood is meant to be a pleasurable experience. It's not a prison where you are locked in with diapers and babies and are not supposed to leave for a breath of fresh air. And don't worry that your kids will detest you for taking some time for yourself. When I was young, the idea of my mother leaving the house without us kids didn't appeal to me. But I understand her now. I realise that we took her for granted and that she deserved to have more time to herself. In fact, if I had a chance to go back in time, I would try and make it up to her. You are not expected to sacrifice your life at the altar of motherhood. So make time for yourself and enjoy it without guilt.

Another thing that keeps you from giving more time to yourself is unnecessary socialising, which I already mentioned earlier. You are the right judge to decide what needs to be a part of your life and what doesn't. Go out with friends you love. Or just laze around with your favourite novel at a local Starbucks. Do whatever you like.

If need be, don't shy away from asking for help from friends and family to watch over your kids so that you can have a respite. You can rotate responsibilities amongst friends to watch the kids all together once or twice a month or whatever suits you. This way, you and your friends all get a chance, and it's fair to everyone.

Rucha Dixit

My husband has always encouraged me to get some "me" time, and it's mutual, so it's worked well for both of us. I hit the gym on a Saturday and Sunday mornings, whereas he plays badminton and tennis with his friends on Sundays and Tuesdays. Having your own space is essential. I am telling you, this will make you a better mother.

MAKE TIME FOR BOTH OF YOU

Just as it's important to make time for yourself, it's also important to spend time with your partner. This ideally means just the two of you spending time, but it doesn't always have to be that way. You can dance together with the children in the background! It can also mean just being present together in the same room doing your own things while the kids are napping. Why not?! Keeping the bond alive is all that is needed, even if it means enjoying the silence together.

Also, try and get family to watch over your kids to get some time together. I don't have that luxury, so we take days off together so we can go out or spend time with each other while the kids are away at school and nursery. It's not possible very frequently, though. If nothing else, we just enjoy a movie together at home after the kids are off to bed.

PLAN AHEAD

Now that you have children, your organisational skills will come in handy. Some are natural-born planners;

others are at the opposite end of the scale, and then there are those who hang in the middle somewhere. Wherever you stand, there is no need to worry, as organising is a skill that can be learnt like any other. A little planning in advance can go far. It can save you a lot of headaches and petulance. All it needs is foresight.

We generally tend to plan for big things and events in life, but what we miss out on is the fact that planning small day-to-day events can make a sea of difference. Every day has a set of routine events which are expected. These are things you can plan for. On a weekday, I know I have to get my children ready for school by 8:30am. So the previous night, I pick clothes for them and me, ready to be worn the next morning. My son wears a school uniform, so not a lot of thinking goes there. But my daughter who goes to preschool doesn't have a uniform, and as she is young, she also needs a set of spare clothes to accompany her. Things like these don't really take a lot of time, but planning saves me a lot of time in the morning when I am busy with a hundred other things.

I usually use my time in the shower or while walking down to work from the train station to plan ahead for things like dinner that night. This might then trigger another thought, though not always, which makes me realise that I need to shop for the necessary ingredients. Then, I can accommodate that shopping at lunchtime. It's so much easier when it's all thought through. If I gave it no thought, then I would stand in the kitchen in the evening wondering what to cook, and worse, realise that I didn't have the ingredients to cook what I would like to.

You definitely know by now that when you have young children, you have a lot of surprises smacking you in the face. But let me tell you a secret: When you have planned for the expected, you are better equipped to handle the unexpected. Like in the above example, initiating the thought is all that was needed, and then the rest just happens automatically. You don't have to worry about the whole bunch of thoughts which occur as a result of thinking that first thought.

It's like when you are travelling in a car at night from London to Birmingham. You don't have to worry about the entire road ahead, stretching hundreds of miles. You have your headlights on and can see a few metres away, and this is enough to take you the entire distance. Your course of action is according to what you see a few metres away. So if you see that the road is bending ahead, then you turn the steering depending on the degree of the bend. And the reason you saw the bend coming is by starting the journey. So the journey begins by hitting the road and, similarly, starting to apply thought ahead of time is what you need to get the ball rolling.

Let's evaluate a situation at its best and worst. First, let's see the unplanned version of a morning and the turn it takes. Say you wake up in the morning, have your coffee, and suddenly realise you haven't filled in a form you have to submit that very same day at your older child's school. You start to fill it in. When you are almost done, your two-year-old wakes up and refuses to leave your lap. You then leave the form half-filled where it is and take your child to the bathroom to brush her teeth. After you are done with that, you go to the wardrobe and start to think about what she will wear to nursery. Once you are through that task and get her dressed, you wonder what breakfast she should have, as she is a fussy eater. Before you know, it she spills a glass of milk on the floor. So now you have the additional task of cleaning up, you have no clue what to feed her, let alone having breakfast ready — and don't forget, you haven't yet filled in the school form.

Did you notice the domino ripple effect? And what does this cause? Delays, frustration, irritability and a whole chain reaction!

Voilà! Now you have a time machine and you can redo this morning by going back in time. You wake up, have your coffee, and as you have given breakfast a thought and decided it's going to be boiled eggs, you put them on the stove while you are sipping coffee. Then, it dawns on you that you have that school form to fill, so you start with the task at hand. In the middle of it, your daughter wakes up. You brush her teeth and get her into the clothes you put out the previous night. You have

41

Rucha Dixit

saved at least 15 minutes by now just by planning ahead. Now, after she spills that glass of milk, you have a task of cleaning it, for sure. But you have her breakfast ready, so you can let your partner feed her that while you clean up. And, finally, you have the 15 or 20 minutes you saved to get back to the form you left incomplete. See the difference? It speaks for itself.

USE TECHNOLOGY

As a mother with young children, there are so many things to deal with at the same time that it's easy to miss something important. For instance, kids' vaccinations; one can't afford to mess up the timing of that. We all use reminders in our phones for this, but the thing is you have to be prompt in adding them and the typing is an additional task that might result in your putting it off until next time. But beware; as a mother, you just have to do certain things when you think of them, because if you wait until next time to do it, something else may come up and you may lose the thought in thin air.

Instead of typing a reminder on your phone, it is more efficient to be able to just speak it into the device. Here are a few useful apps for setting reminders. All of them are similar in terms of how you use them. You can speak into your phone, asking it to remind you about doing ABC on day XYZ at time EFG and watch your phone ring at EFG on XYZ to remind you to do ABC.

1. Siri on your iPhone.

42

2. S Voice App on Samsung Galaxy Phones.
3. Google Now, which is for both iOS and Android.

These tools and applications have been around, and I am not saying I am the first one to use them. You may be using them already. But I still think they need mentioning as they might help you discover something new and help you to make use of its full potential.

PRAY & LET GO

We are human, and we all have bad days! Even after practising all this, there are days when I just can't cope with so much thrown at me. Children getting sick, lack of energy, job responsibilities, emotional ups and downs, etc.

You might think, "What is she talking about? Prayer? Isn't that the call of the helpless?" No, it's not. The power of prayer is highly underestimated and underrated. It's so simple that our ego refuses to accept this amenity we have at our disposal. Surrendering to God or the divine, or whatever way you would like to label the supreme power, takes true grit. Ask for physical strength, mental strength or whatever you want. Ask, and you will be given. So don't hold back in prayer.

CHAPTER 5. LESSONS LEARNT AT PARENTING SCHOOL

These are a few things I found effective with my kids. Most of these are generic. I am not trying to tell you I am perfect and that this is the way it should be. That's rubbish. You might have found your own ways that are equally effective, but I will be glad if these tips and tricks help you discover something new. I still have my moments of imperfection, but even just being aware of yourself can significantly improve situations and make for more effective parenting. And that's where transformation starts, with awareness.

BECOME WHAT YOU WANT TO TEACH YOUR KIDS

"What you do speaks so loudly that I cannot hear what you say."

–Ralph Waldo Emerson

After my son was a year and a few months old, one of his favourite lines was, "Nnnoooooo." He would stress the "No" so much, with his finger pointing to me. Guess where he learnt it? From me! And that day I learnt something. Not to never say "No," as that is needed occasionally. But to become that which I wanted him to learn.

Kids are very good observers. They silently observe everything you do and say, and also everything you don't say, through your body language. And this starts at a very young age.

If you want them to listen to you, start listening to them.

If you want them to share, then start sharing.

If you want them to be polite and soft-spoken, then mind your own manners.

If you want them to evolve into people with moral values, then…

…You get it by now, don't you?

Imagine little Diana, watching her favourite TV show when her daddy gets a phone call. Now, Diana's dad is completely insensitive to the fact that she is enjoying her show and carries on talking loudly to his friend instead of leaving the room. She gets hushed off if she tries to say anything. Now, when this situation is flipped around years later when Diana has grown into a young woman, can Diana's dad expect her to show him some consideration and leave the room when she gets a call on her mobile while he is watching his favourite program and doesn't want to be disturbed? He probably will, and if he doesn't get it, he might even make it a point to strongly show his disapproval of her behaviour. But what he has missed is the fact that he unknowingly taught her to be like that.

Rucha Dixit

You can force your children to behave in a certain way, but is that what you want? Even if that works, it will be superficial. But watching you behave in the way they are being asked to will reinforce the message.

I heard a lovely talk the other day by Brahmakumari Sister Shivani. She said that punishing or reacting with anger cannot head anyone in the right direction. The intention should be transformation so that the mistake isn't repeated in the future, not humiliation. Punishment is for something that has already happened, and so it is futile. On the contrary, it can lead to creating rebellion and enforcing that trait in a person instead of curing it. So it is with children, too.

She shared the experience of one of the women who was in the audience a few days back. This woman had a three-year-old who was very upset about being left at home when she wanted to accompany her mum to this seminar. So she threw a tantrum and cried when her mum got home. As a part of being on this course, this lady was asked not to get angry for the next three days. What she would have done on a usual day was to scream at her child and leave her crying. But since they had been asked not to express anger, she sat with her bawling child, telling her repeatedly that she would take her along the next day. She kept her tone calm even when her daughter was throwing her hands and legs about, and even when she could feel the anger inside her erupting. But she had promised herself not to let it

46

out that day. In 15 minutes, her daughter calmed down, started to talk in a tone that matched her mother's, and eventually hugged her. This lady choked as she said, "Today, I realised how I can change her by changing myself."

The change you seek begins with you. Lead by example.

RESPECT IS MUTUAL

Your child is a soul who has come to you in the form of your child. Realising this changes the equation in the parent-child relationship. Even a child deserves to be respected.

Now, respect has different forms, and it's not the way you respect people older to you. It's about respecting their feelings, keeping your promises, nurturing their self-respect and not crushing their egos. I am not suggesting being overly polite, plastic and saying "yes" to everything. It is important and necessary at times to say "no" to your kids. But the way you do that is what matters. As a parent, it's easy to find yourself in an authoritative position, but keeping a check on yourself can help. Beware of slamming your child's ego to make your point. This defeats the purpose and instead creates rebels.

Respecting them will earn you respect. You can't expect to get what you don't give, can you? Remember, what goes around, comes around.

ROLE-PLAYS

Little role-plays are a fun way of teaching younger children. The way I realised this was through watching them play with each other and with friends. I was pleasantly surprised by all the wisdom my son was spilling out, very much in contradiction to his behaviour sometimes.

Say my son screams at my daughter who is waiting for her turn to have the iPad from him. It's surely not right, and not fair, either. In situations like these, when I get a chance, I put them in a role-play the next time their friends are at home. I ask him to play "Daddy," get my daughter to play herself and the friend to play my son, who is not being fair by keeping the iPad to himself and not sharing it with his sister. So what does my son do now? He gets into Daddy's shoes and this changes his perspective. Guess what? He becomes the big wise Daddy who tries to get his daughter to have a fair chance at playing with the iPad. Surprising, isn't it?

It might be difficult, though, to convince them to always take your role-play scenario suggestions on board!

DIVERSIONS WORK

At the times when children just won't listen to you and get adamant about doing what they want, try diverting them instead of refusing repeatedly. It works most of the time — if not for long, at least for some time — and it definitely takes the edge off an unpleasant situation.

Not only does it divert your kid, it also diverts you, especially if you are on the verge of losing your mind and blowing your top.

My husband is very good at this. When we are "under cry attack" — that is, when my children are howling at the tops of their voices, suddenly he comes up with a question out of the blue about their favourite TV show character or something completely tangential to the situation. And they just forget about crying and answer the question! This works with those under six, but I doubt it will beyond that age.

EMPHASISING A POINT

It's necessary to tell your children that they are wrong when they are. But sometimes it's difficult to get your point across, especially with young children, because they can get very much occupied with crying and not understand what you are trying to say to them. At that stage, it's better to leave the situation if you see you aren't succeeding in making your point. Instead, in a situation like that what I do is bring it up when my children are in a good mood and try explaining it to them when they appear more receptive. This prevents the original scene from getting ugly and also makes sure that my point is taken on board.

LOVE IS POWERFUL

I tell my kids often that I love them and that I am for them when they need me. It's not necessarily verbal.

Actions speak for themselves and are louder than words. Hugs, kisses and cuddles work! It's important to emphasize this message, as it is a child's source of strength and sound backing. That's the way I was brought up and now I am giving it forward.

Children who bully others at school, who get involved in drugs and crime, or even those who commit suicide are very likely to be suffering from lack of love. They are victims themselves. Love heals. It can radically reduce the youth suicide rate.

My friend recently told me about her friend, who I will call Sally, who had a very difficult teenager to deal with. She told me that Sally was in despair and didn't know where she went wrong. Her daughter would scream at her and revolt at everything she said and did. It got so bad that they had to go for counselling. When the counsellor spoke to Sally's daughter, she realised how unloved felt this young lady, who didn't even remember her mother, Sally, hugging her. When the counsellor told Sally about this, Sally was shocked. She said that she loved her daughter with all her heart but just wasn't that expressive. This realisation magically metamorphosed their relationship and now they are best friends.

Difficult circumstances and children can make you skilful, and don't forget to harness the power of love.

APPRECIATE

Recognition and appreciation works not only at work, but also at home.

Don't forget to appreciate and recognise any good act or positive character attributes displayed by your child. It injects them with the impetus to do more of it. I generally do stickers or draw them five stars on their hands. You can come up with your own ways to appreciate. See how their faces light up.

LISTEN AND ENCOURAGE COMMUNICATION

We are all very preoccupied with ourselves amidst the hustle and bustle of modern life. Keeping an open ear can help. Children say a lot of things that can provide powerful feedback to you as a parent and tell you the way they perceive you and the things around them. It's also a way to tap into information, which helps you make sure they are on track.

For instance, encouraging them to talk about their days in school is a good way to keep track of what's happening in their lives when you are not present with them. We do it every day at bedtime, and all credit goes to my husband for starting it. We reciprocate by telling them what we did at work. It keeps the conversation interesting and casual. It also shows them that we are interested and will go a long way in developing a rapport with them. So the younger you start, the better.

CHAPTER 6. LEARNING FROM CHILDREN

Children are manifestations of innocence and purity. Keeping your mind open during interactions with your kids can expose you to a world of wisdom. The virtues that I will talk about are more prevalent under the age of four. As they grow beyond that point, ego and intellect start kicking in and that's where the decline begins.

Just watching my kids has given me so much insight into how pure we are when we come into the world. It makes me wonder what makes us lose the spark.

ENTHUSIASM IS ABUNDANT

My daughter can literally dance with joy when I open a packet of candy in front of her. I remember how excited I used to be on seeing my dad pick me up from school every Friday at five years of age. I met him then just like my daughter, who scurries into my arms when I get home. Sounds familiar, right?

When do you last remember being over-ecstatic at the idea of having ice cream or jumping with excitement on seeing your friends? Probably when you were four or five, or even up until 10 years of age. Does the idea of watching a movie excite you anymore? Probably if you are a teenager, or even a young adult, but not so much for a 65-year-old. Well, you may not be a movie buff, and that's not what I am implying you should be. But the capacity to derive joy out of small things diminishes as we age.

Why does this joyfulness dampen? Most of us don't even smile that often, and we mostly talk about our problems, let alone hop around with happiness. You might think, "Well, kids don't have to deal with problems." You are forgetting how little problems seemed big when you were very young. Happiness is a choice you make.

UNCONDITIONAL LOVE & FAITH

Children love unconditionally. Have you seen a baby lying in the arms of its mother? That is a moment of pure bliss. I read a beautiful quote the other day that said, "Trust should be like the feeling of a one-year-old baby; when you throw him in the air, he laughs, because he knows you will catch him." As a child, my sister used to hold on to my mother's hand and cross the road with her eyes closed because the vehicles used to scare her. She had complete trust in my mother.

Most adults have forgotten to trust each other, let alone having faith in God, whom you can't even see. Even when someone pays us a compliment, it makes us think, if they want something from us in return or if they genuinely mean it. Doubt has clouded our minds and every aspect of our lives.

LIVING IN THE MOMENT

I have yet to find a three-year-old who sits and worries about what he will become in the future or what he will wear for a party. Kids are ever-present; they are engrossed watching television, playing with friends, or painting, busy in the activity at hand. Even when they cry, it's about something that happened in that moment. I can't remember my children sobbing away thinking about how I told them off last week. They don't carry baggage from the past. But as we grow, we start accumulating unpleasant memories from the past and hold grudges.

This is one of the most profound lessons I have taken from them. It's one of the hardest to do, but the rewards are equally worthy.

NON-JUDGEMENTAL AND TRANSPARENT

Have you noticed how easily you smile at a baby or a child you have never seen before? We have all seen someone do this or done it ourselves. Adults rarely smile at strangers but don't hesitate to make funny, twisty, smiley faces at other children. That's because children don't judge but adults do.

Our judgment hats go on as soon as we meet someone. And conversely, we are always wary of being judged. We are mostly consumed with worry about what others think about us. When we meet someone, we make an impression about that person; in other words, a screen is created in our minds. From that moment onwards, anything that person says or does is seen through that screen. So if a person has created a positive impression in our mind and we like him or her, then a little wrongdoing from that person is perceived as insignificant and we let go of it. On the other hand, if it's a screen of negativity we hold for someone, then every act is perceived negatively.

Kids fight and quarrel but get over it, then and there. They are much more transparent about their feelings and emotions. And the best part is that they openly talk to each other when in a fight instead of backbiting. Their equations are simpler.

CHILDREN DON'T FEEL THE NEED TO CONTROL

Most of us, or actually all of us, are control freaks. We want to hold on to the reins of every aspect of our lives. And for that, we manipulate, lie, and betray.

Just watch how a two-year-old has surrendered to his parents. He knows that whatever is being done is in his best interest. He takes whatever comes his way without finding the need to control or change the situation. Can't we give God that pleasure by being in a state of surrender? And let me tell you, this isn't an indication of an absence of strength but actually is a sign of colossal strength. To have the patience to let things take their time to unfold is strength, of course!

Rucha Dixit

There is nothing wrong about learning from your own children. Making a choice to be a student all your life will enrich not only your life, but also the lives of others around you. We all should feel free to tap into the wisdom children display and take away life lessons.

Chapter 7. Meditation For Children

Doesn't the way things are going these days scare you? Murder, gun crime, sexual abuse — and what is worse, the increasing involvement of youth in such horrendous crimes. Unfortunately, it's news like this that's making headlines these days. According to the World Health Organisation, a staggering 350 million people on this planet have been diagnosed with depression. That is slightly over four percent of the world's population.

What many lack is self-love. It's astounding how many people can't look themselves in the mirror and feel love for themselves. How is it possible to love others if one can't love oneself? No wonder the suicide rate is skyrocketing. Where are we all heading towards? Is this the type of environment we want our future generations to thrive in?

Wouldn't you want your child and everyone to live in a beautiful world where crime ceased, hatred perished and love prevailed? What we don't realise is that we have the potential to create it. Stop waiting for someone to come and transform everything and magic this world into an ideal place. Being a parent is a blessing, and a blessing in many ways, of which this is one. As a parent, you have been bestowed that power and opportunity to create that world. How? You hold the seeds to the future. If you sow love, future generations will reap love. If each of us plays our part well, then that day isn't far away when fear will cease to exist and love and trust will persist.

It's a shame that we take pride in violence. What do the movies show our young people? They promote the concept of "being cool" in the form of the hero who smashes and kills and wounds. That is the definition of coolness. But the fact is someone who is able to remain calm and composed in the face of insult is cool. Someone who is able to forgive and let go and not react but respond is cool, is the real hero, and is the quintessence of strength. But how many of us are actually convinced of this, convinced enough to pass this on to younger minds?

"If every eight-year-old in the world is taught meditation, we will eliminate violence from the world within one generation."

-Dalai Lama

You might think about how meditation solves the problem of violence. Violence exists not only in actions, but also in thoughts, and that's where it starts: in the mind. The fact is that even though most of us aren't criminals, the reasons we aren't are because we know that it's morally wrong and because we know we will face consequences, not necessarily because we don't feel like it. Yes, we shouldn't do violence, and it's good most of us don't get involved in such acts. But we choose not to for the wrong reasons. Do you see the difference? It's subtle! What matters is intention. And if we were to be arrested for intention, a significant chunk of the population on this planet would be behind bars.

That's where meditation helps. It can curb negative tendencies, aggression or anger of any kind. So getting kids to do it is an excellent way to nip it in the bud. Meditation should be a part of the school curriculum. It deserves to be a significant part of the education system, and not having it only highlights a flaw. We would have happier youth today if they were taught how to handle their minds. As per The Guardian Newspaper, the ChildLine, part of the NSPCC (The National Society for the Prevention of Cruelty to Children), which is a charity campaign working in child protection in the UK, registered an 87% rise in calls about cyber-bullying last year, a 41% increase in calls about self-harm, and a 33% increase in calls about suicide, with the biggest increase among 12- to 15-year-olds. Self-harm sites and depression blogs are a trend amongst the youth these days. And it's not only in the UK; it's the same story pretty much everywhere.

What we teach our kids is to compete with each other and to be better than each other rather than being better than themselves. We teach them to hit back if they get hit, instead of teaching them to forgive and love. We teach them that success is to acquire more than everyone — more money, more material things — instead of emphasizing that true success is the ability to smile through everything in life. This is ignorance. And truly, as Martin Luther King Jr. said, *"Nothing in the world is more dangerous than sincere ignorance and conscientious stupidity."* Education is not only meant to enable one to read and do math, which are necessary, of course. But true education is to develop and empower young minds to be able to see the larger picture instead of dwelling in small thinking. When I say "larger picture," I mean the fact that everyone is connected and that we all originate from the same divine power, and hence hurting others is as bad as hurting ourselves.

So I would like to have you consider the fact that meditation is much needed for everyone, especially our children, because children are our future and we need a strong foundation to build a solid world of morals ahead of us.

A further positive point is that meditation cleanses and sharpens the mind and increases creativity, and this means it can help your child get better grades in school with less effort as it increases the ability to focus. Children are quick learners. If you practise it regularly, it will become a norm as they watch you meditate.

Only once I started regularly meditating did I realise what I had missed all these years. But time gone never comes back. So why waste it? I certainly plan to introduce my kids to meditation so they are exposed to its benefits early on, and you certainly won't regret doing the same.

Chapter 8. Remember, It Will Pass

I was flying from London once to visit my parents when my daughter was just three months and my son was two-and-a-half years old. My husband couldn't accompany me. It was going to be a long, hard journey and I was a little nervous to handle them without his help. After security check, I received a text message from my husband. It read, "Have a safe flight and take care. And when it gets too hard, remember one thing, it will pass!"

That is the most profound and beautiful text message I have ever received. It left me smiling. I felt a sense of relief dawning on me as I thought, "Yeah, that's right. It will end; it has to. Then, why worry?!"

How easily we forget this truth, both in happiness and in anguish. No matter how hard you try, neither can you hold on to a good situation nor can you hold on to a bad phase of life, as they both have to pass in their own time.

I remember when my daughter wasn't born by her due date. I couldn't wait to give birth. I was so desperate to get it done with that I opted for acupressure as a way to induce labour. When she was born, I felt she was better off in my tummy, where I didn't have to bother feeding her explicitly every two hours. Moreover, handling two kids and sleep deprivation had taken a toll on me. I just couldn't understand why I had to rush it. Even if it meant a few extra days of peace, it would have been worth having. But I didn't see that side when I was in the waiting phase.

Have you heard mothers talking about how difficult it is to take care of a newly born baby, and that they can't wait for it to grow up? When the baby grows up into a toddler who starts running around, falling over, and making a mess around the house, they probably find themselves missing the two-month-old bundle of joy that used to stay put wherever you placed it without even turning. That's not possible, anyway, so now they can't wait for the child to grow up and be independent. With independence, the child develops a head of its own. And guess what? That isn't easy either. So, the truth is that every stage has its own pros and cons. But the important thing is to see the upside in the present instead of looking to the past or the future, and to remember that it shall pass, too. Every time I get saturated with a situation, I just remind myself how lucky I am to have my lovely children and that I should enjoy every bit of this time with them.

So enjoy the good while it lasts. Let go of the frustration, anger or any negative sentiment and remind yourself that this, too, shall pass. In the spur of the moment, don't express yourself in a way that you might regret later. Enjoy every moment, because your child's childhood won't come back. You can make a career when they are grown, earn more money later, and will have more free time on your hands to do whatever you like. But moments full of innocence, toothless giggles, clumsy-wobbly walks and falls, carefree laughter, wonder-struck eyes and immensely blissful hugs won't come back. This, too, shall pass!

CHAPTER 9. GOODBYE AND GOOD LUCK

Well, there it is. I hope this made you feel like you had company in all your ups and downs, and that you are not the only one going through this phase of life. And I hope it has helped you understand how you can overcome some of the snags of being a new mum, as well as discover some new things.

Here's to your newly acquired motherhood!

INSPIRATIONAL BOOKS, ARTICLES & VIDEOS

Dr. Wayne Dyer's Blog on "Why the Inside Matters"

http://www.drwaynedyer.com/blog/why-the-inside-matters

"The Enlightened Parent," by Dr. Wayne Dyer

http://www.healyourlife.com/author-dr-wayne-w-dyer/2011/06/lifeshelp/intuitive-guidance/the-enlightened-parent

E-Squared: Nine Do-It-Yourself Energy Experiments That Prove Your Thoughts Create Your Reality, by Pam Grout

http://amzn.to/1f0ix9a

E-Squared Experiment 3, demonstrated to prove that each of us is surrounded by an electromagnetic field

http://youtu.be/yXVnapkyN8M

BBC: Meditation 'good for brain'

http://news.bbc.co.uk/1/hi/health/2725487.stm

BBC: Scans 'show mindfulness meditation brain boost'

http://www.bbc.co.uk/news/health-16406814

Daily Affirmations by Louise Hay

http://www.louisehay.com/affirmations/

Don't Lose Your Mind, Lose Your Weight by Rujuta Diwekar

http://amzn.to/1bTK1HF

I Can Do It: How to Use Affirmations to Change Your Life by Louise Hay

http://amzn.to/1dOroJv

BEFORE YOU GO...

I hope you enjoyed this book. If you can take a little time to write me a review, I will give you a big hug!

I would love to hear from you if you think this book helped you in any way, and also if you have any suggestions or comments. Please visit Amazon and post your review.

Your feedback and support always matter.

Many thanks,

Rucha

Printed in Great Britain
by Amazon

13978469R00047